WHAT IS DATA SCIENCE?

DR. SURESH KUMAR RUDRAHITHLU

This book is dedicated to my parents Late R.S.Yadapadithaya Shishila and Late Premalatha

Contents

CHAPTER ONE

Big Data Analytics:

The volume of data that one has to deal has exploded to unimaginable levels in the past decade, and at the same time, the price of data storage has systematically reduced. Private companies and research institutions capture terabytes of data about their users' interactions, business, social media, and also sensors from devices such as mobile phones and automobiles. The challenge of this era is to make sense of this sea of data. This is where big data analytics comes into picture

Big Data Analytics largely involves collecting data from different sources, mange it in a way that it becomes available to be consumed by analysts and finally deliver data products useful to the organization business.

Big Data Life Cycle:

A big data analytics cycle can be described by the following stage –

· Business Problem Definition
· Research
· Human Resources Assessment
· Data Acquisition
· Data Munging
· Data Storage
· Exploratory Data Analysis
· Data Preparation for Modelling and Assessment
· Modelling
· Implementation
· Data Munging
· Data Storage
· Exploratory Data Analysis
· Data Preparation for Modelling and Assessment
· Modelling
· Implementation

Data formats:

Data can mean many different things, and there are many ways to classify it. Two of the more common are:

§ Primary and Secondary: Primary data is data that you collect or generate. Secondary data is created by other researchers, and could be their primary data, or the data resulting from their research.

§ Qualitative and Quantitative: Qualitative refers to text, images, video, sound recordings, observations, etc. Quantitative refers to numerical data. There are typically five main categories that it can be sorted into for management purposes. The category that you choose will then have an effect upon the choices that you make throughout the rest of your data management plan.

Data formats:

Data can mean many different things, and there are many ways to classify it. Two of the more common are:

§ Primary and Secondary: Primary data is data that you collect or generate. Secondary data is created by other researchers, and could be their primary data, or the data resulting from their research.

§ Qualitative and Quantitative: Qualitative refers to text, images, video, sound recordings, observations, etc. Quantitative refers to numerical data. There are typically five main categories that it can be sorted into for management purposes. The category that you choose will then have an effect upon the choices that you make throughout the rest of your data management plan.

Data formats:

Data can mean many different things, and there are many ways to classify it. Two of the more common are:

§ Primary and Secondary: Primary data is data that you collect or generate. Secondary data is created by other researchers, and could be their primary data, or the data resulting from their research.

§ Qualitative and Quantitative: Qualitative refers to text, images, video, sound recordings, observations, etc. Quantitative refers to numerical data. There are typically five main categories that it can be sorted into for management purposes. The category that you choose will then have an effect upon the choices that you make throughout the rest of your data management plan.

Data formats:

Data can mean many different things, and there are many ways to classify it. Two of the more common are:

§ Primary and Secondary: Primary data is data that you collect or generate. Secondary data is created by other researchers, and could be their primary data, or the data resulting from their research.

§ Qualitative and Quantitative: Qualitative refers to text, images, video, sound recordings, observations, etc. Quantitative refers to numerical data. There are typically five main categories that it can be sorted into for management purposes. The category that you choose will then have an effect upon the choices that you make throughout the rest of your data management plan.

Missing Data:

Missing data is always a problem in real life scenarios. Areas like machine learning and data mining face severe issues in the accuracy of their model predictions because of poor quality of data caused by missing values. In these areas, missing value treatment is a major point of focus to make their models more accurate and valid.

Types of missing data:

Understanding the reasons why data are missing is important for handling the remaining data correctly. If values are missing completely at random, the data sample is likely still representative of the population. But if the values are missing systematically, analysis may be biased. For example, in a study of the relation between IQ and income, if participants with an above-average IQ tend to skip the question _What is your salary?‘, analyses that do not take into account this missing at random may falsely fail to find a positive association between IQ and salary. Because of these problems, methodologists routinely advise researchers to design studies to minimize the occurrence of missing values. Graphical models can be used to describe the missing data mechanism in detail.

Types of Data Transformation:

Batch Data Transformation:

Traditionally, data transformation has been a bulk or batch process,whereby developers write code or implement transformation rules in a data integration tool, and then execute that code or those rules on large volumes of data. This process can follow the linear set of steps as described in the data transformation process above.

Batch data transformation is the cornerstone of virtually all data integration technologies such as data warehousing, data migration and application integration

When data must be transformed and delivered with low latency, the term —micro batch is often used. This refers to small batches of data (e.g. a small number of rows or small set of data objects) that can be processed very quickly and delivered to the target system when needed.

Benefits of Batch Data Transformation:

Traditional data transformation processes have served companies well for decades. The various tools and technologies (data profiling, data visualization, data cleansing, data integration etc.) have matured and most (if not all) enterprises transform enormous volumes of data that feed internal and external applications, data warehouses and other data stores.

Limitations of Traditional Data Transformation:

This traditional process also has limitations that hamper its overall efficiency and effectiveness.

The people who need to use the data (e.g. business users) do not play a direct role in the data transformation process. Typically, users hand over the data transformation task to developers who have the necessary coding or technical skills to define the transformations and execute them on the data.

This process leaves the bulk of the work of defining the required transformations to the developer. The developer interprets the business user requirements and implements the related code/logic. This has the potential of introducing errors into the process (through misinterpreted requirements),

and also increases the time to arrive at a solution.

Interactive Data Transformation:

Interactive data transformation (IDT)is an emerging capability that allows business analysts and business users the ability to directly interact with large datasets through a visual interface, understand the characteristics of the data (via automated data profiling or visualization), and change

or correct the data through simple interactions such as clicking or selecting certain elements of the data.

Although IDT follows the same data integration process steps as batch data integration, the key difference is that the steps are not necessarily followed in a linear fashion and typically don't require significant technical skills for completion.

A number of companies, primarily start-ups such as Trifacta, Alteryx and Paxata provide interactive data transformation tools. They are aiming to efficiently analyze, map and transform large volumes of data without the technical and process complexity that currently exists

IDT solutions provide an integrated visual interface that combines the previously disparate steps of data analysis, data mapping and code generation/execution and data inspection.IDT interfaces incorporate visualization to show the user patterns and anomalies in the data so they can identify erroneous or outlying values.

Once they've finished transforming the data, the system can generate executable code/logic, which can be executed or applied to subsequent similar data sets.

By removing the developer from the process, IDT systems shorten the time needed to prepare and transform the data, eliminate costly errors in interpretation of user requirements and empower business users and analysts to control their data and interact with it as needed.

The Data Mining Process:

This is a simple analytical process which you will continuously need to refine. Once you get to one stage, you will almost certainly find that you need to go back a step and refine some more before you finally get the data into a format that you can use. Business Understanding > Data Understanding > Data Preparation > Analysis and Modeling> Evaluation > Deployment.

Exploratory data analysis:

In statistics, exploratory data analysis (EDA) is an approach to analyzing data sets to summarize their main characteristics, often with visual methods. A statistical model can be used or not, but primarily EDA is for seeing what the data can tell us beyond the formal modeling or hypothesis testing task. Exploratory data analysis is a concept developed by John Tuckey (1977) that consists on a new perspective of statistics. Tuckey's idea was that in traditional statistics, the data was not being explored graphically, it was just being used to test hypotheses. The first attempt to develop a tool

was done in Stanford, the project was called prim9. The tool was able to visualize data in nine dimensions, therefore it was able to provide a multivariate perspective of the data.

In recent days, exploratory data analysis is a must and has been included in the big data analytics life cycle. The ability to find insight and be able to communicate it effectively in an organization is fuelled with strong EDA capabilities.

Descriptive Analysis:

Descriptive statistics are used to describe the basic features of the data in a study. They provide simple summaries about the sample and the measures. Together with simple graphics analysis, they form the basis of virtually every quantitative analysis of data.

Descriptive statistics are typically distinguished from inferential statistics. With descriptive statistics you are simply describing what is or what the data shows. With inferential statistics, you are trying to reach conclusions that extend beyond the immediate data alone. For instance, we use inferential statistics to try to infer from the sample data what the population might think. Or, we use inferential statistics to make judgments of the probability that an observed difference between groups is a dependable one or one that might have happened by chance in this study. Thus, we use inferential statistics to make inferences from our data to more general conditions; we use descriptive statistics simply to describe what's going on in our Exploratory data analysis data.

Descriptive Statistics are used to present quantitative descriptions in a manageable form. In a research study we may have lots of measures. Or we may measure a large number of people on any measure. Descriptive statistics help us to simplify large amounts of data in a sensible way. Each descriptive statistic reduces lots of data into a simpler summary. For instance, consider a simple number used to summarize how well a batter is performing in baseball, the batting average. This single number is simply the number of hits divided by the number of times at bat (reported to three significant digits). A batter who is hitting .333 is getting a hit one time in every three at bats. One batting .250 is hitting one time in four. The single number describes a large number of discrete events. Or, consider the scourge of many students, the Grade Point Average (GPA). This single number describes the general performance of a student across a potentially wide range of course experiences.

Every time you try to describe a large set of observations with a single indicator you run the risk of distorting the original data or losing important detail. The batting average doesn't tell you whether the batter is hitting home runs or singles. It doesn't tell whether she's been in a slump or on a streak. The GPA doesn't tell you whether the student was in difficult courses or easy ones, or whether they were courses in their major field or in other disciplines. Even given these limitations, descriptive statistics provide a powerful summary that may enable comparisons across people or other units.

Univariate Analysis:

Univariate analysis involves the examination across cases of one variable at a time. There are three major characteristics of a single variable that we tend to look at:

§ the distribution

§ the central tendency

§ the dispersion

In most situations, we would describe all three of these characteristics for each of the variables in our study.

The Distribution: The distribution is a summary of the frequency of individual values or ranges of values for a variable. The simplest distribution would list every value of a variable and the number of persons who had each value. For instance, a typical way to describe the distribution of college

students is by year in college, listing the number or percent of students at each of the four years. Or, we describe gender by listing the number or percent of males and females. In these cases, the variable has few enough values that we can list each one and summarize how many sample cases had the value. But what do we do for a variable like income or GPA? With these variables there can be a large number of possible values, with relatively few people having each one. In this case, we group the raw scores into categories according to ranges of values. For instance, we might look at GPA according to the letter grade ranges. Or, we might group income into four or five ranges of income values. Frequency distribution table.

One of the most common ways to describe a single variable is with a frequency distribution. Depending on the particular variable, all of the data values may be represented, or you may group the values into categories first (e.g., with age, price, or temperature variables, it would usually not be sensible to determine the frequencies for each value. Rather, the value are grouped into ranges and the frequencies determined.). Frequency distributions can be depicted in two ways, as a table or as a graph.

Central Tendency: The central tendency of a distribution is an estimate of the "centre" of a distribution of values. There are three major types of estimates of central tendency:

§ Mean

§ Median

§ Mode

The Mean or average is probably the most commonly used method of describing central tendency. To compute the mean all you do is add up all the values and divide by the number of values. For example, the mean or average quiz score is determined by summing all the scores and dividing by

the number of students taking the exam. For example, consider the test score values: 15, 20, 21, 20, 36, 15, 25, 15

The sum of these 8 values is 167, so the mean is 167/8 = 20.875

The Median is the score found at the exact middle of the set of values. One way to compute the median is to list all scores in numerical order, and then locate the score in the centre of the sample. For example, if there are 500 scores in the list, score #250 would be the median. If we order the 8

scores shown above, we would get: 15, 15,15,20,20,21,25,36

There are 8 scores and score #4 and #5 represent the halfway point. Since both of these scores are 20, the median is 20. If the two middle scores had different values, you would have to interpolate to determine the median.

The mode is the most frequently occurring value in the set of scores. To determine the mode, you might again order the scores as shown above, and then count each one. The most frequently occurring value is the mode. In our example, the value 15 occurs three times and is the model. In some distributions there is more than one modal value. For instance, in a bimodal distribution there are two values that occur most frequently

Notice that for the same set of 8 scores we got three different values -- 20.875, 20, and 15 -- for the mean, median and mode respectively. If the distribution is truly normal (i.e., bell-shaped), the mean, median and mode are all equal to each other

Dispersion:

Dispersion refers to the spread of the values around the central tendency. There are two common measures of dispersion, the range and the standard deviation. The range is simply the highest value minus the lowest value. In our example distribution, the high value is 36 and the low is 15, so the range is 36 - 15 = 21.

The Standard Deviation is a more accurate and detailed estimate of dispersion because an outlier can greatly exaggerate the range (as was true in this example where the single outlier value of 36 stands apart from the rest of the values. The Standard Deviation shows the relation that set of scores has to the mean of the sample. Again let's take the set of scores: 15, 20,21,20,36,15,25,15 To compute the standard deviation, we first find the distance between each value and the mean

CHAPTER TWO

What is Data Science?

Introduction:

What can data science do? What characteristics distinguish data science from previous scientific discovery paradigms? What are the methods for conducting data science? What is the impact of data science? This chapter offers initial answers to these and related questions. A companion chapter (Brodie, 2018b) addresses the development of data science as a discipline, as a methodology, as well as data science research and education. Let's start with some slightly provocative claims concerning data science. Data science has been used successfully to accelerate discovery of probabilistic outcomes in many domains. Piketty's (2014) monumental result on wealth and income inequality was achieved through data science. It used over 120 years of sporadic, incomplete, observational economic data, collected over ten years from all over the world (Brodie, 2014b). What is now called computational economics was used to establish the correlation, with a very high likelihood (0.90), that wealth gained from labor could never keep up with wealth gained from assets. What made front page news worldwide was a second, more dramatic correlation that there is a perpetual and growing wealth gap between the rich and the poor. This second correlation was not derived by data analysis but is a human interpretation of Piketty's data analytic result. It contributed to making Capital in the 21st Century the best-selling book on economics, but possibly the least read. Within a year, the core result was verified by independent analyses to a far greater likelihood (0.99). One might expect that further confirmation of Piketty's finding would be newsworthy; however, it was not as the more dramatic rich-poor correlation, while never analytically established had far greater appeal. This illustrates the benefits and risks of data science. Frequently, due to the lack of evidence, economic theories fail. Matthew Weinzierl, a leading Harvard University economist, questions such economic modelling in general saying, "that the world is too complicated to be modelled with anything like perfect accuracy" and "Used in isolation, however, it can lead to trouble" (Economist, February 2018). Reputedly, Einstein said: "Not everything that counts can be counted. Not everything that's counted, counts". The hope is that data science and computational economics will provide theories that are fact-based rather than based on hypotheses of "expert" economists (Economist, January 2018) leading to demonstrably provable economic theories, i.e., what really happened or will happen. This chapter suggests that this hope will not be realized this year.

Many such outcomes2 have led to verified results through methods outside data science. Most current data analyses are domain specific, many even specific to classes of models, classes of analytical methods, and specific pipelines. Few data science methods have been generalized outside their original domains of application, let alone to all domains (to illustrated in a moment). A rare and excellent exception is a generic scientific discovery method over scientific corpora (Nagarajan et. al., 2015) generalized from a specific method over medical corpora developed for drug discovery (Spangler et. al., 2014) that is detailed later in the chapter. It is often claimed that data science will transform conventional disciplines. While transformations are underway in many areas, including supply chain management3 (Waller and Fawcett, 2013) and chemical engineering (Data Science, 2018), only time and concrete results will tell the extent and value of the transformations. The companion chapter On Developing Data Science (Brodie, 2018b) discusses with the transformation myth. While there is much science in many domain-specific data science activities, there is little fundamental science that is applicable across domains. To warrant the designation data science, this emerging paradigm requires fundamental principles and techniques applicable to all relevant domains, just as the scientific principles of the scientific method apply across many domains. Since most data science work is domain specific, often model- and method-specific, data science does not yet warrant the designation as a science. This chapter explores the current nature of data science, its qualitative differences with its predecessor scientific discovery paradigms, its core value and components that, when mature, would warrant the designation data science. Descriptions of large-scale data science activities referenced in this chapter apply, scaled down, to data science activities of all sizes, including increasingly ubiquitous desktop data analytics in business.

What is Data Science?

What is data science? Due to its remarkable popularity, there is a plethora of descriptions of data science, for example: Data Science is concerned with analyzing data and extracting useful knowledge from it. Building predictive models is usually the most important activity for a Data Scientist4 . Data Science is concerned with analyzing Big Data to extract correlations with estimates of likelihood and error. (Brodie, 2015a) Data science is an emerging discipline that draws upon knowledge in statistical methodology and computer science to create impactful predictions and insights for a wide range of traditional scholarly fields5 . Due to data science being in its infancy, these descriptions reflect some of the many contexts in which it is used. This is both natural and appropriate for an emerging discipline that involves many distinct disciplines and applications. A definition of data science requires the necessary and sufficient conditions that distinguish it from all other activities. While such a definition is premature, a working definition can be useful for discussion. The following definition is intended to explore the nature of this remarkable nediscovery paradigm. It is based on studying over 150 data science use cases and benefits from three years research and experience over a previous version (Brodie, 2015a). Like many data science definitions, it will be improved over the next decade in which data science will mature and gain the designation as a new science. Data Science is a body of principles and techniques for applying data analytic methods to data at scale, including volume, velocity, and variety, to accelerate the investigation of phenomena represented by the data, by acquiring data, preparing and integrating it, possibly integrated with existing data, to discover correlations in the data, with measures of likelihood and within error bounds. Results are interpreted with respect to some predefined (theoretical, deductive, top-down) or emergent (fact-based, inductive, bottom-up) specification of the properties of the phenomena being investigated. A simple example of a data science analysis is the pothole detector developed at MIT (Eriksson et. al., 2008) to identify potholes on the streets of Cambridge, MA. The data was from inexpensive GPS and accelerometer devices placed in a fleet of taxis that drive over Cambridge streets. The model was designed ad hoc for this application. A model consists of the features (i.e., variables) essential to the analysis and the relationships amongst the features. It was developed in this case ad hoc by the team iteratively refining the model through imagination, observation, and analysis. Ultimately, it consisted of a large number of movement signatures, i.e., model features, each designed to detect specific movement types that may indicate potholes and non-potholes, e.g., manholes, railroad tracks6 , doors opening and closing, stopping, starting, accelerating, etc. Additionally, the size of the pothole was estimated by the size of the movement. The analytical method was the algorithmic detection and filtering of non-pothole signatures leaving as a result those movements that correlate with potholes with an estimated severity, likelihood, and error bound. The severity and likelihood estimates were developed ad hoc based on verifying some portion of the detected movements with the corresponding road surfaces thus contributing to estimating the likelihood that the non-potholes were excluded, and potholes were included. Error bounds were based on the precision of the equipment, e.g., motion device readings, network communications, data errors, etc. The initial result was many thousands of locations with estimated severities, likelihoods, and error bounds. Conversion of likely pothole locations (correlations) to actual potholes severe enough to warrant repair (causal relationships between movements and potholes) were estimated by a manual inspection of some percentage of candidate potholes. The data from the inspection of the actual locations, called ground truth, was used to verify the likelihood estimates and establish a threshold above which confidence in the existence of a pothole warranted sending out a repair crew to repair the pothole. The customer, the City of Cambridge, MA, was given a list of these likely potholes. The immediate value of the pothole detector was that it reduced the search for potholes from manually inspecting 125 miles of roads and relying on citizen reports that takes months, to discovering 6 The pothole models consist of a number of signature movements, i.e., abstractions used to represent movements of the taxi, only some of which are related to the road surface. Each signature movement was created using the data (variables or features) available from a smartphone including the clock for time, the GPS for geographic location (latitude and longitude), and the accelerometer to measure changes in velocity along the x, y, and z axes. For example, the taxi crossing a railroad track would result in many signature "single tire crossing single rail line" movements, one for each of four tires crossing each of several rail lines. A "single tire crossing single rail line" involves a sudden, short vertical (x-axis) acceleration combined with a short lateral (y-axis) movement, forward or backward, with little or no lateral (z-axis) movement. Discounting the railroad crossing as a pothole involves recognizing a large number of movements as a taxi is crossing a rail line - all combinations of "single tire crossing single rail line" forward or backward, at any speed, and at any angle - to determine the corresponding staccato of the multiple single tire events over multiple lines. The pothole model is clearly ad hoc, in contrast to well established models in physics and retail marketing likely, sever potholes within days of their creation. Since 2008, pothole detectors have been installed on city vehicles in many US cities. The pothole detector team created Cambridge Mobile Telematics that develops applications for vehicles sensor data, e.g., they annually produce reports on distracted driving across the USA based on data from over 100 million trips (Cambridge Mobile Telematics, 2018). While these applications were used initially by insurance companies they are part of the burgeoning domain of autonomous vehicles and are being used by the US National Academy of Sciences (Dingus T.A., 2016) for driving safety. 3 Data science is a new paradigm of discovery Data science emerged from, and has many commonalities with, its predecessor paradigm, the scientific method7 ; however, they differ enough for data science to be considered a distinct, new paradigm. Like the scientific method, data science is based on principles and techniques required to conduct discovery activities that are typically defined in terms of a sequence of steps, called a workflow or pipeline; results are specified probabilistically and with error bounds based on the data, the model, and the analytical method used; and the results are interpreted in terms of the hypothesis being evaluated, the model, the methods, and the probabilistic outcome relative to the accepted requirements of the domain of the study. In both paradigms, models are collections of features (represented by variables that determine the data to be collected) that characterize the essential properties of the phenomenon being analyzed. Data corresponding to the features (variables) in the model are collected from real instances of the phenomena and analyzed using analytical methods developed for the type of analysis to be conducted and the nature of the data collected, e.g., different methods are required for integers uniformly distributed in time versus real numbers skewed due to properties of the phenomenon. The outcomes of the analysis are interpreted in terms of the phenomena being analyzed within bounds of precision and errors that result from the data, model, and method compared with the precision required in the domain being analyzed, e.g., particle physics requires precision of six standard deviations (six sigma). Data science differs paradigmatically from the scientific method in data, models, methods, and outcomes, as described below. Some differences may be due to data science being in its infancy, i.e., models for real-time cyberattacks may not yet have been developed and proven; however, some differences, discussed below, are inherent. We are in the process of learning which is which.

Data science data, models, and methods Data science data is often obtained with limited knowledge of the conditions under which the data was generated, collected, and prepared for analysis, e.g., data found on the web; hence, it cannot be evaluated as in a scientific experiment that requires precise controls on the data. Such data is called observational. Compared with empirical scientific data, data science data is typically, but not necessarily, at scale by orders of magnitude in one or more of volume, velocity, and variety. Scale requires management and analytic methods seldom required in empirical science. Data science models used in most scientific domains have long histories of development, testing, and acceptance, e.g., the standard model of particle physics8 emerged in 1961 after decades of development and has matured over the subsequent decades. In contrast, currently data science models, e.g., for real-time bidding for online advertising, are created on demand for each data science activity using many different, innovative, and ad hoc methods. Once a model is proven, they can be accepted and Another practical example is at Tamr.com that offers one of the leading solutions for curating or preparing data at scale, e.g., data from 100,000 typically heterogeneous data sources. It launched initially with a comprehensive solution in the domain of information services. Tamr soon found that every new domain required a substantial revision of the machine learning component. Initially, like most AI-based startups, their initial solution was not generalizable. As can be seen at Tamr.com, Tamr now has solutions in many domains for which they have substantial commonality in the underlying solutions. Another fundamental difference between science and data science concerns the scale and nature of the outcomes. The scientific method is used to discover causal relationships between a small number of variables that represent the essential characteristics of the natural phenomena being analyzed. The experimental hypothesis defines the correlation to be evaluated for causality. The number of variables in a scientific experiment is kept small due to the cost of evaluating a potentially vast number of combinations of variables of interest. PhD theses, i.e., an experiment conducted by one person, are awarded on experiments with two or three but certainly less than ten variables. Large-scale experiments, e.g. LIGO13, Kepler14, and Higgs-Boson, may consider 100s of variables and take years and thousands of scientists to evaluate. Determining whether a correlation between variables is causal tends to be an expensive and slow process. Data science, on the other hand, is used to rapidly discover as many correlations between the data values as exist in the data set being analyzed, even with very large models (millions of variables) and vast data sets. Depending on the analytical method used, the number of variables in a data science analysis can be effectively unlimited, e.g., millions, even billions, as can be the number of correlations between those variables, e.g., billions or trillions. Data science analytics are executed by powerful, efficient algorithms using equally powerful computing infrastructure (CPUs, networks, storage). The combined power of new algorithms and infrastructure in the 1990's led to the current efficacy of machine learning that in turn contributed to the emergence of data science.

The prime benefit of data science is accelerating discovery Data science and empirical science differ dramatically, hence paradigmatically, in the scale of the data analyzed. Scientific experiments tend to evaluate a small number, e.g., 10s or 100s, of correlations to determine if they are causal, and do so over long periods of time, e.g., months or years. In contrast, data science can identify effectively unlimited numbers of correlations, e.g., millions, billions, or more, in short time periods, from minutes to days. It is in this sense that data science is said to accelerate discovery. Originally developed in the 1990's for scientific discovery, the remarkable results of data science have resulted in its being applied to all endeavors for which adequate data is available. The prime benefit of data science is that it is a new paradigm for accelerating discovery, in general. Ideally, data science is used to accelerate discovery by rapidly reducing a vast search space to a small number of correlations that are likely to be casual, as indicated by their estimated probability. Depending on the resources available, some number of the probabilistic correlations are selected to be analyzed for causality by well-established (non-data science) means in the domain being analyzed. For example, data science has been used to accelerate cancer drug discovery. The Baylor-Watson study (Spangler et. al., 2014) used data science methods to identify nine likely cancer drug candidates. It used a simple, novel method to further evaluate their likelihood. The original analysis was conducted over drug research results published up to 2003 and identified nine likely candidate drugs. The likelihood of those nine candidate drugs was raised significantly when the research published from 2003 to 2013 showed that seven of the nine candidates had been validated as genuine cancer drugs. This raised the likelihood that the remaining two candidate drugs were real. Standard EPA-approved drug development and clinical trial testing were then used to develop the two new drugs. In this case, data science accelerated drug discovery for a specific type of cancer. It started with a vast search space of cancer research results from 240,000 papers. In three months it discovered the two highly likely cancer drug candidates. Conventionalcancer drug discovery typically discovers one drug every two to three years. These times do not include the drug development and clinical trial periods. 3.4 Causal reasoning in data science is complex and can be dangerous Just as the scale is radically different so is the nature of the results. The scientific method discovers results that, if executed correctly, are definitive, i.e., true or false, with a defined probability and error bound, that a hypothesized relationship is causal. Data science discovers a potentially large number of correlations each qualified by a probability and error bound that indicate the likelihood that the correlation may be true. Data science is used to discover correlations; it is rarely used to determine causal relationships. The previous sentence is often misunderstood not just by novices, but also, unfortunately, by data scientists. Empirical science discovers causal relationships in one step. Data science is frequently used to discover causal relationships in two steps: First, discover correlations with a strong likelihood of being causal; then use non-data science methods to validate causality. Causality is the Holy Grail of science, scientific discovery, and if feasible, of data science. Typically, the goal of analyzing a phenomenon is to understand Why some aspects of the phenomenon occur, for example, why does it rain? Prior to a full understanding of the phenomenon, initial discovery is often used to discover What conditions prevail when the phenomenon manifests, e.g., as rain starts and during rain many raised umbrellas can be observed. A more informed observer may also discover specific climatic conditions. All of the conditions observed to be present consistently before and during the rain could be said to be correlated with rain. However, correlation does not imply causation, e.g., raised umbrellas may be correlated with rain, but do not cause the rain (Brodie, 2014a). A more realistic example comes from an online retailer that observing that increased sales were correlated with customers purchasing with their mobile app, invested significantly to get their app onto many customers' smartphones. However, the investment was lost since sales did not increase. Increased purchases were correlated with mobile apps on customers' smartphones; however, the causal factor was customer loyalty and, due to their loyalty, most loyal customers already had the app on their smartphones. Data Science is used predominantly to discover What. Empirical science and many other methods are used to discover Why (Brodie, 2018a). Data science is often used to rapidly reduce the search space from a vast number of correlations or possible results to a much smaller number. The much smaller number of highly probable results are then analyzed with non-data science methods, such as scientific experiments or clinical trials, to verify or reject the result, i.e., automatically generated hypotheses, as causal. There are mathematics and methods claimed for deducing causal effects from observational data (i.e., data not from controlled experiments but from surveys, censuses, administrative records, and other typically uncontrolled sources such as in Big Data and data science). They are very sophisticated and require a deep understanding of the mathematics, statistics, and related modelling methods. Judea Pearl has developed such methods based on statistics, Bayesian networks, and related modelling, see (Pearl, 2009a,b,c). For decades, statisticians and econometricians have developed such methods with which to estimate causal effects from observational data, since most social and economic data is purely observational (Winship et. al., 1999). Causal reasoning involves going beyond the mathematics and modelling for data science in which correlations are obtained. "One of Pearl's early lessons is that it's only possible to draw causal conclusions from observational (correlational) data if you are willing to make some assumptions about the way that the data were sampled and about the absence of certain confounding influences. Thus, my understanding is that one can draw causal conclusions, but it's important to remember that these are really conditional on the validity of those assumptions." says Peter Szolovits, Professor, CSAIL, MIT, with a decade of experience applying data science in medical contexts

Finding correlations between variables in (Big) data together with probabilities or likelihoods of the correlation occurring in the past or future, are relatively easy to understand and safe to report. Making a causal statement can be misleading or dangerous depending on the proposed actions to be taken as a consequence. Hence, I do not condone nor confirm causal reasoning; it is above my pay grade; hence, I quote experts on the topic rather than make my own assertions. I recommend that causal reasoning not be applied without the required depth of knowledge and experience, because making causal statements as a result of data science analysis could be dangerous. In lecturing on correlation versus causation for over five years, I have found that an inordinate amount of interest is given to this difficult and little understood topic, perhaps with a desire to be able to provide definitive answers, even when there are none. I have found no simple explanation. You either study, understand, and practice causal reasoning with the appropriate care or simply stay away until you are prepared. Experts are appropriately cautious. "I have not, so far, made causal claims based on my work, mainly because I have not felt strongly enough that I could defend the independence assumptions needed to make such claims. However, I think the kinds of associational results are still possibly helpful for decision makers when combined with intuition and understanding. Nevertheless, I think most clinicians today do not use predictive models other than for more administrative tasks such as staffing or predicting bed occupancy" – Peter Szolovits, MIT. "I firmly believe that [deriving] causal results from observational data is one of the grand challenges of the data science agenda!" – David Parkes, co-lead of the Harvard Data Science Initiative. "Pearl once explained those ideas to me personally at Santa Catalina workshop, but I still don't fully understand them either :)" – Gregory Piatetsky-Shapiro, President of KDnuggets, co-founder of KDD Conferences and ACM SIGKDD

Data science flexibility:

Data-driven or hypothesis-driven Empirical science and data science have another fundamental difference. The scientific method uses deductive reasoning, also called hypothesis-driven, theory-driven, and top-down. Deductive reasoning is used when specific hypotheses are to be evaluated against observations or data. A scientific experiment starts by formulating a hypothesis to be evaluated. An experiment is designed and executed, and the results interpreted to determine if the hypothesis is true or false under the conditions defined for the hypothesis. It is called theory-driven in that a theory is developed, expressed as a hypothesis, and an experiment designed to prove or invalidate the hypothesis. It is called top-down since the experiment starts at the top – with the idea – and goes down to the data to determine if the idea is true. Data science can be hypothesis-driven. That is, as with empirical science, a data science activity can start with a hypothesis to be evaluated. Unlike empirical science, the hypothesis can be stated with less precision and the models, methods, and data can be much larger in scale, i.e., more variables, data volume, velocity, and variety. In comparison, data science accelerates discovery by rapidly reducing a vastly larger search space than would have been considered for empirical methods, to a small set of likely correlations; however, unlike empirical science, the results are correlations that require additional, nondata science methods to achieve definitive, causal results. One of the greatest advantages of data science is that it can discover patterns or correlations in data at scale vastly beyond human intellectual, let alone temporal, capacity; far beyond what humans

could have conceived. Of course, a vast subset of those found may be entirely spurious. Data science can use inductive reasoning, also called bottom-up, data-driven, or fact-based analysis, not to evaluate specific hypotheses but using an analytical model and method to identify patterns or correlations that occur in the data with a specific frequency. If the frequency meets some predefined specification, e.g., statistical significance in the domain being analyzed, it can be interpreted as a measure of likelihood of the pattern being real. As opposed to evaluating pre-defined hypotheses in the theory-driven approach, the data-driven approach is often said to "automatically" generate hypotheses, as in (Nagarajan, 2015). The inductive capacity of data science is often touted as its magic as the machine or methods such as machine learning, "automatically" and efficiently discover likely hypotheses from the data. While the acceleration and the scale of data being analyzed are major breakthroughs in discovery, the magic should be moderated by the fact that the discovered hypotheses are derived from the models and methods used to discover them. The appearance of magic may derive from the fact that we may not understand how some analytical methods, e.g., some machine learning and deep learning methods, derive their results. This is a fundamental data science research challenge as we would like to understand the reasoning that led to a discovery, as is required in medicine, and in 2018 in the European Union, by law (the General Data Protection Regulation (GDPR16))

Data science is in its infancy The excitement around data science and its many successes are wonderful, and the potential of data science is great, but these positive signs can be misleading. Not only is data science in its infancy as a science and a discipline, its current practice has a large learning curve related largely to the issues raised above. Gartner, Forrester, and other technology analysts report that most (80%) early (2010-2012) data science projects in most US enterprises failed. In late 2016, Gartner reported that while most enterprises declare data science as a core expertise, only 15% claim to have deployed big data projects in their organization (Gartner, 2016). Analysts predict 80+% failure rate through 2017 (Demirkan & Dal, 2014) (Veeramachaneni, K. 2016) (Lohr & Singer, 2016). 3.7 It's more complicated than that Data science methods are more sophisticated than the above descriptions suggest, and datadriven analyses are not as pure. Data science analytical methods and models do not discover any and all correlations that exist in the data since they are discovered using algorithms and models that incorporate some hypotheses that could be considered biases. That is, you discover what the models and methods are designed to discover. One must be objective in data science across the entire workflow - data selection, preparation, modelling, analysis, and interpretation; hence, a data scientist must always Doubt and Verify (Brodie, 2015b). It may be useful to experiment with the models and methods. When a data science analysis reduces a vast search space, it (or the observing human) may learn something about the discovered correlations and may warrant an adjustment and re-running the model, the method, or even adjusting the data set. Hence, iterative learning cycles may increase the efficacy of the analysis or simply provide a means of exploring the data science analysis search space. Top-down and bottom-up analytical methods can be used in combination, as follows. Start with a bottom-up analysis that produces N candidate correlations. Select a subset of K of the correlations with an acceptable likelihood and treat them as hypotheses to be evaluated. Then use them to run hypothesisdriven data science analyses and determine, based on the results, which hypotheses are again the most likely or perhaps even more likely than the previous run and discard the rest. These results can be used in turn to redesign the data science analysis, e.g., iteratively modify the data, model, and method, and repeat the cycle. This approach is used to explore data, models, and methods - the main components of a data science activity. This method of combining top-down and bottom-up analysis has been proposed by CancerCommons, as a method for accelerating the development of cancer cures as part of the emerging field of translational medicine.

Data science components :

Extending the analogy with science and the scientific method, data science, when mature, will be a systematic discipline with components that are applicable to most domains – to most human endeavors. There are four categories of data science components, all emergent in the data science context awaiting research and development: 1) principles, data, models, and methods; 2) data science pipelines; 3) data science infrastructure; and 4) data infrastructure. Below, we discuss these components in terms of their support of a specific data science activity. Successful data science activities have developed and deployed these components specific to their domain and analysis. To be considered a science, these components must be generalized across multiple domains, just as the scientific method applies to most scientific domains, and in the last century has been applied to domains previously not considered scientific, e.g., economics, humanities, literature, psychology, sociology, and history.

Data science principles, data, models, and methods A data science activity must be based on data science principles, models, and analytical methods. Principles include those of science and of the scientific method applied to data science, for example, deductive and inductive reasoning, objectivity or lack of bias relative to a given factor, reproducibility, and provenance. Particularly important are collaborative and cross-disciplinary methods. How do scientific principles apply to discovery over data? What principles underlie evidence-based reasoning for planning, predicting, decision-making, and policy-making in a specific domain? In May 2017, the Economist declared, on its front cover, that data was The World's Most Valuable Resource (Economist, May 2017). Without data there would be no data science or any of its benefits. Data management has been a cornerstone of computer science technology, education, and research for over 50 years, yet Big Data that is fueling data science, is typically defined as data at volumes, velocities, and variety that cannot be handled by data management technology. A simple example is that data management functions in preparing data for data analysis take 80% of the resources and time for most data science activities. Data management research is in the process of flipping that ratio so that 80% of resources can be devoted to analysis. Discovering data required for a data science activity whether inside or outside an organization is far worse. Fundamental data research is required in each step of the data science pipeline to realize the benefits of data science. A data science activity uses one or more models. A model represents the parameters that are the critical properties of the phenomenon to be analyzed. It often takes multiple models to capture all relevant features. For example, the LIGO experiment, that won the 2017 Nobel Prize in Physics for empirically establishing the existence of Einstein's gravitational waves, had to distinguish movement from gravitational waves from seismic activity and 100,000 other types of movement. LIGO required a model for each movement type so as to recognize it in the data and discard it as gravitational wave activity. Models are typically domain specific, e.g., seismic versus sonic, and are often already established in the domain. Increasingly, models are developed specifically for a data science activity, e.g., feature extraction from a data set is common for many AI methods. Data science activities often require the continuous refinement of a model to meet the analytical requirements of the activity. This leads to the need for model management to capture the settings and results of the planned and evaluated model variations. It is increasingly common, as in biology, to use multiple, distinct models, called an ensemble of models, each of which provides insights from a particular perspective. Each model, like each person in Plato's Allegory of the Cave, represents a different perspective of the same phenomenon, what Plato called shadows. Each model – each person – observes what appears to be the same phenomenon, yet each sees it differently. No one model – person – sees the entire thing, yet collectively they capture the whole phenomenon from many perspectives. It may also be that a critical perspective is missed. It is rarely necessary, feasible, or of value to integrate different perspectives into a single integrated model. After all, there is no ultimate or truthful model save the phenomenon itself. Ensemble or shadow modelling is a natural and nuanced form of data integration (Liu, 2012) analogous to ensemble modelling in biology and ensemble learning (Dietterich, 2000) and forecasting in other domains. A data science activity can involve many analytical methods. A given method or algorithm is designed to analyze specific features of a data set. There are often variations of a method depending on the characteristics of the data set, e.g., sparse or dense, uniform or skewed, data type, data volume, etc., hence methods must be selected, or created, and tuned for the data set and analytical requirements, and validated. In an analysis, there could be as many methods as there are specific features with corresponding specific data set types. Compared with analytical methods in science, their definition, selection, tuning, and validation in data science often involves scale in choice and computational requirements. Unless they are experts in the related methods, it is unlikely that a practicing data scientist understands the analytical method, e.g., a specific machine learning approach, that they are applying relative to the analysis and data characteristics, let alone the thousands of available alternatives. Anecdotally, I have found that many practicing data scientists use the algorithms that they were taught rather than selecting the one most applicable to the analysis at hand. There are significant challenges in applying sophisticated analytical models and methods in business (Forrester, 2015). Having selected or created and refined the appropriate model, i.e., collection of features that determine the data to be collected, collected and prepared the data to comply with the requirements of the model, and selected and refined the appropriate analytical method, the next challenge is interpreting the results and, based on the data, model, and method, evaluate the likelihood, within relevant error bounds, that the results are meaningful hypotheses worthy of validating by other means

Data science workflows or pipelines:

The central organizing principle of a data science activity is its workflow or pipeline and its life cycle management (NSF, 2016). A data science pipeline is an end-to-end sequence of steps from data discovery to the publication of the qualified, probabilistic interpretation of the result in the form of a data product. A generic data science pipeline, such as listed below, is comprehensive of all data science activities, hence can be used to define the scope of data science. 1. Raw data discovery, acquisition, preparation, and storage as curated data in data repositories 2. Selection and acquisition of curated data from data repositories for data analysis 3. Data analysis 4. Results interpretation 5. Result publication and optionally operationalize the pipeline for continuous analyses The state of the art of data science is such that every data science activity has its own unique pipeline, as each data science activity is unique. Due to the emergence and broad applicability of data science, there is far more variation across data science pipelines than across conventional science pipelines. Data science will benefit, as it develops, from a better understanding of pipelines and guidance on their design and development. Data science pipelines are often considered only in terms of the analytics, e.g., the machine learning algorithms used to derive the results in step 3. However, most of the resources required to design, tune, and execute a data science activity are required not for data analysis, steps 3 and 4 of a data science pipeline, but for the design and development of the pipeline and for steps 1 and 2. The design, development, and tuning of an end-to-end pipeline for a data science activity typically poses significant data modelling, preparation, and management challenges often requiring significant resources and time required to develop and execute a data science activity. Two examples are astrophysical experiments, the Kepler Space Telescope launched in 2009 to find exoplanets and Laser Interferometer Gravitational-Wave Observatory (LIGO) that was awarded the 2017 Nobel Prize in Physics. Initial versions of the experiments failed not because of analysis and astrophysical aspects and models, but due to the data pipelines. Due to unanticipated issues with the data, the Kepler Science Pipeline had to be rewritten (Jenkins, 2010) while Kepler was inflight retaining all data for subsequent corrected processing. Similarly, earth-based LIGO's pipeline was rewritten (Singh, 2007) and renamed Advanced LIGO. Tuning or replacing the faulty pipelines delayed both experiments by approximately one year. Once the data has been acquired, the most time-consuming activity in developing a pipeline was data preparation. Early data science activities in 2003 reported 80-90% of resources devoted to data preparation (Dasu & Johnson, 2003). By 2014 this was reduced to 50-80% (Lohr, 2014). In specific cases, this cost negatively impacted some domains (Reimsbach-Kounatze, 2015) due to the massive growth of acquired data. As data science blossomed so did data volumes, leading experts in 2015 to analyze the state of the art and estimating that data preparation typically consumed 80% of resources (Castanedo, 2015). By then products to curate data at scale, such as Tamr.com, were maturing and being more widely adopted. Due to the visibility of data science, the popular press surveyed data scientists to confirm the 80% estimates (Press, 2016; Thakur 2016). In 2017, technical evaluations of data preparation products and their use again identified the 2003 estimates of 80% (Mayo, 2017) (Gartner G00315888, 2017)

www.ingramcontent.com/pod-product-compliance
Ingram Content Group UK Ltd.
Pitfield, Milton Keynes, MK11 3LW, UK
UKHW061828190726
13853UKWH00009B/2498

9 798886 672411